A PICTURE HISTORY OF BRITISH RAIL

Diesels and Electrics in Action

G. M. KICHENSIDE

DAVID & CHARLES

NEWTON ABBOT   LONDON   NORTH POMFRET (VT)   VANCOUVER

Railway history in pictures series
Midlands by H. C. Casserley and C. C. Dorman
North-East England by K. Hoole
North-West England by J. A. Patmore and J. Clark
Wales and the Welsh Border Counties by H. C. Casserley
The West Country by R. C. Riley
Ireland Vols 1 and 2 by A. MacCutcheon
Scottish by John Thomas
The Somerset & Dorset Railway by Robin Atthill
The Stockton & Darlington Railway by K. Hoole
Wessex by H. C. Casserley

ISBN 0 7153 7168 1
Library of Congress Catalog Card Number

© David & Charles 1976

Printed in Great Britain
by Biddles Limited Guildford
for David & Charles (Publishers) Limited
Brunel House Newton Abbot Devon

Published in the United States of America
by David & Charles Inc
North Pomfret Vermont 05053 USA

Published in Canada
by Douglas David & Charles Limited
1875 Welch Street North Vancouver BC

Contents

	Introduction	5
1	The pioneers	11
2	Electrics inherited — NER and LMR	16
3	Electrics inherited — Southern	23
4	BR diesel locomotives	29
5	Diesel multiple-units	58
6	1500 volt dc electrics	64
7	Great Eastern electrics	65
8	West Coast electrics	69
9	The Southern in the seventies	74
10	The freight revolution	79
11	Servicing the fleet	85
12	New stations for old	86
13	Signalling for speed	88
14	Air-conditioned comfort	91
15	Improving the track	92
16	Trains of tomorrow	94
	BR diesel and electric locomotive classification	96

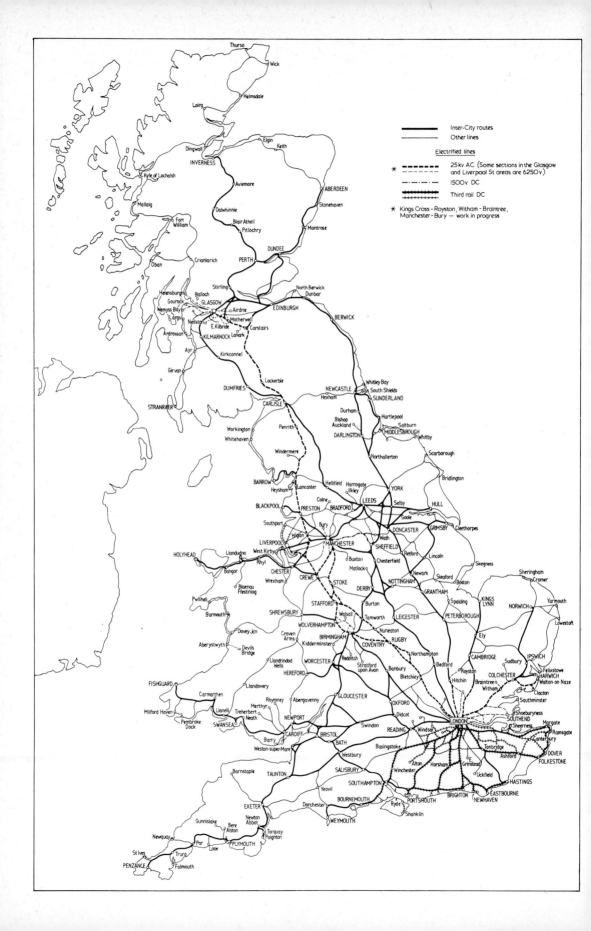

Introduction

To many enthusiasts diesel and electric traction are modern developments in railway technology, largely because British Railways opted for these forms of power rather later than railway administrations in other parts of the world. Yet electricity took its first unsteady steps (or should it be revolutions) for rail use almost at the start of railways, when just over 130 years ago a vehicle was made to move by the power of electricity derived from cells fed to an electro-magnet which attracted iron plates attached to the axles and caused the wheels to revolve. Nothing more really came of the idea until a means of generating electricity from a dynamo had been perfected, and, moreover, ways of transmitting that power from the ground or the track to the vehicle were evolved. Werner von Siemens is generally accepted to have tried out the first electric locomotive in 1879 when he successfully demonstrated a narrow gauge machine which picked up current from the track fed from a lineside dynamo.

Similarly internal combustion engines of one sort or another occupied the attention of numerous engineers right through the Victorian era but it was not until the 1870s that the petrol engine began to emerge as a practicable possibility and a decade or so later when the oil engine began to show promise. Although the oil engine is always associated with the German engineer Rudolf Diesel—indeed his name has stuck as the generic description for the type—he was only one of several engineers who took out patents for oil engines. In Britain by the late 1880s the Priestman oil engine had been developed for use in powering pumps, machines, etc, and the first Priestman engine installed in a railway vehicle, a small four-wheel tractor, was built in 1894. It was of 12hp and used for shunting wagons; it was the first of many lightweight shunters built for service in industry and elsewhere from then on by various manufacturers. The first large high-power locomotives were really developments by European engineers, particularly Swiss and German firms. The main problem though was the transmission of power to the wheels since internal combustion engines have no torque on starting and cannot be used with a direct drive to the wheels like a steam engine. The first large main line locomotive built with a Swiss compression ignition engine in 1912 was designed with direct drive but had to be started by compressed air to get the locomotive under way. It was a dismal failure and the era of the heavy locomotive for main line work really did not start until transmission problems had been solved with the development of suitable electric or hydraulic equipment in the 1920s and 1930s since clutch and gearbox or other forms of mechanical drive were suited only to low power units. The story of the development of the internal combustion locomotive is almost as fascinating as that of the steam locomotive and is described more fully in *The British Internal-Combustion Locomotive 1894-1940* by Brian Webb published by David & Charles.

Despite the pioneering work in diesel and electric traction during the decades around the turn of the century, and the opening of the first suburban and underground electric railways between 1890 and 1915 the steam locomotive remained supreme in Britain largely because it was simple to make and cheap to operate. Electrification was expensive particularly because of the cost of power distribution to the trains and the amount of lineside equipment needed to boost supplies to avoid voltage drop, and diesel locomotives had not reached a stage where they could be used on heavy long-distance trains, at least not by the 1920s.

The turning point came in the early 1930s when the LMS carried out experiments with diesel locomotives, employing various types of transmission, for shunting purposes in marshalling yards. Eventually electric transmission seemed to offer the most efficient form and in the mid- and late-1930s the LMS placed orders for production batches of diesel shunters. The Great Western meanwhile had introduced a batch of diesel passenger railcars for branch and main line stopping services, in which the power equipment followed very much the latest thinking in bus building practice. Although a few suburban lines around London and some provincial cities had been electrified before the first world war, mostly with direct current (dc) at about 600 volts supplied by a third, or third and fourth rail, it was the Southern Railway which turned to large scale electrification for its suburban services in the 1920s and 1930s, and extended to its main lines to Brighton, Portsmouth and other South Coast towns before the second world war. Two lines electrified in 1908/9—the Lancaster, Morecambe & Heysham, and the LBSCR South London lines—used overhead catenary supply carrying high voltage 6600 volts alternating current (ac), while the North Eastern Railway used 1500 volts dc with overhead catenary supply for its Newport-Shildon freight line in 1915.

ELECTRIFICATION—THE OVERHEAD SYSTEMS

During the 1930s the 1500V dc overhead system was made the future electrification standard but it was applied to only three routes, Manchester-Altrincham in 1931, Manchester-Sheffield/Wath including the Glossop branch in 1954 and the Liverpool Street-Shenfield-Southend/Chelmsford routes in 1949/56. In the mid 1950s trials in France and Germany were showing that high voltage alternating current using up to 25,000V at the industrial frequency of 50 cycles (Hz) was more economic to install and run than 1500V dc, and with the development of modern more-efficient types of rectifier to convert ac to dc suitable for traction motors (technical problems even today limit the use of ac motors for traction use where standard 50Hz supply is employed), British Railways changed its policy in 1956 to use this form of electrification for the future. Moreover where later extensions of electrification were made to 1500V dc lines it was on the new 25,000V ac system and the original 1500V dc equipment was adapted and converted to work from high voltage ac. This occurred particularly on the lines from Liverpool Street to Southend and Chelmsford, converted to the alternating current system when the main line to Colchester and Clacton was electrified. Indeed the Clacton line was used as a proving ground for the 25,000V ac system. To save renewing all the original 1500V catenary equipment and providing additional clearances around live wires needed for the 25,000V system the former 1500V lines are fed at 6250V ac. Thus electric trains on lines from Liverpool Street have a changeover switch to work on either 25,000 or 6250V ac. The change from one voltage to the other is made automatically as the train passes the meeting point between the two voltages by magnets on the track which initiate the switching of train equipment.

Glasgow area lines are also subdivided into these two voltages in the same way not because of a conversion but because of tunnel sections where insulation clearances for 25,000V were thought to be impossible to attain. The main reason is that at 25,000V a clear air space (originally 11in but later reduced to 8in) is required round live wires to avoid any possibility of a flashover to adjoining equipment or

6

structures. This is why it is dangerous to go very close to or place objects near overhead live wires, because a shock, often fatal, might be received without actually touching the wires.

In the normal way the system is perfectly safe but not when children trespassing on the railway climb overhead equipment supports, or dangle anything over the edge of bridge parapets. Bridges on lines electrified with overhead catenary are raised to stop such dangerous practices but nothing is really proof against a determined child.

Undoubtedly the most ambitious electrification project carried out by British Railways as part of modernisation undertaken over the last 20 years has been the West Coast main line from Euston to Glasgow. Work started in the mid 1950s and the first section was opened from Manchester to Crewe in 1960; further stages followed to Liverpool and gradually southwards to Euston completed in 1966. The Birmingham area followed a year later and then came the decision to go for Glasgow, completed in 1974 and providing a 400-mile electrified trunk route carrying passenger trains over most of its length at speeds of 100mph.

MAIN LINE DIESELISATION

But what of other routes? The 1955 modernisation plan, which envisaged the eventual elimination of steam traction, proposed the introduction of diesel locomotives to principal routes, as an interim measure on those to be electrified and as the main source of power on other lines. Thus the East Coast route from Kings Cross to Edinburgh (originally considered for early electrification but later shelved), the Midland line from St Pancras to Carlisle and Glasgow, and Western Region routes from London to the West of England and South Wales would all be diesel worked. A pilot scheme for a small number of diesel locomotives from several manufacturers was put in hand immediately but even before the prototypes could take to the rails in 1957/8 bulk orders for more were placed which resulted in a proliferation of types, so that even today no fewer than five types in the 2000-2750 horse power (hp) range are at work when one common type could have covered all the varying duties. The Western Region did not help matters when it went its own way in developing a fleet of lightweight locomotives (78 tons in the case of the Swindon Warship class of 2000hp) with hydraulic transmission based on German practice instead of the heavier locomotives (133 tons of the English Electric 2000hp type) with diesel driven generators and electric transmission favoured by the rest of BR and British industry.

By the mid 1960s it was clear which types of locomotive were the best in terms of reliability, maintenance needs, and running costs and a national traction plan was evolved to eliminate the designs deemed to be unsuitable or non-standard as electrification extensions were commissioned and threw up some diesel locomotives as surplus. As a result some BR diesel types had very short lives, a few as little as five years. The smaller types were often sold to industrial lines to replace old steam locomotives for shunting duties. In contrast one or two classes, particularly the English Electric type 1s of class 20 and the type 4s of class 40 are nearing 20 years of service. The various class designations and numbering of BR diesel and electric stock are described elsewhere in this book.

Most BR diesel types are used fairly widely over the system and there is usually no physical reason why one class cannot work on similar duties on similar lines anywhere in the country but in fact because of the variety of types specific classes are often allocated to one or two depots for maintenance so that stocks of spares can

7

be rationalised. For example surviving WR diesel-hydraulic locomotives are allocated to Plymouth Laira depot but in practice may be seen over most parts of the WR and occasionally on through workings to other regions. Other factors are also involved though, including the type of automatic warning system (aws) equipment fitted to the locomotive (for many years the WR-based locomotives were fitted only with the former GWR mechanical contact aws), whether it has electric train heating, and whether it has air brakes in addition to vacuum brakes. Until the early 1960s vacuum brakes were standard on all BR locomotive-hauled passenger trains and those freight trains that had power brakes but BR then opted for a change to compressed air brakes which are faster in application and release, and provide greater braking force in more-compact equipment, and are more suited to high speeds. Thus during the last decade BR operation has been bedevilled by the variety of train equipment during the changeover period and sometimes problems have arisen when a locomotive fitted with one type of equipment has inadvertently been sent out to work a train in which the coaches have another type. Unfortunately it was one of those unavoidable difficulties with which the operators have had to live if BR was to take advantage of modern technology, but it was a pity that the decision to change could not have been taken at the start of the modernisation programme in the mid-1950s to coincide with the introduction of diesel and electric traction.

One of the most widely used types of locomotive is the Brush/Sulzer class 47 which can be found at work on most parts of BR, even occasionally on through workings to the nearly all-electric Southern Region. In contrast the 22 Deltic class 55 locomotives are confined almost entirely to the East Coast main line on express passenger workings between Kings Cross, Leeds, Newcastle and Edinburgh since they were designed and built specifically for these services, and were the first diesel locomotives intended for regular working at 100mph. The Deltics were the outcome of an experimental locomotive (now preserved in the Science Museum, London) built by the English Electric Co as a demonstration machine. Other manufacturers built prototype locomotives to show off their products to BR, which later resulted in the Brush/Sulzer class 47s and the English Electric class 50s. Now BR is venturing into higher power locomotives with a batch of 3750 horse power machines intended for freight work on order and due for delivery from 1976 to replace earlier types.

MULTIPLE-UNIT TRAINS

For non-electrified local services on main lines, suburban routes and branches the 1955 modernisation plan provided for diesel multiple-unit trains, that is fixed formation trains of two, three or four coaches, with driver's cabs at both ends, and diesel engines under the coaches driving the wheels through a fluid clutch and gear-box equipment. When accelerating, the driver changes gear as speed rises, more or less as on a bus. When traffic is heavy several units of this type each with their own power can be coupled together to make longer trains but all under the control of one driver in the front cab. The term multiple-unit refers to these self-contained trains which can run in multiple, under the control of one driver. Electric trains with electric motors on the coaches, similarly are called electric multiple-units, and again can be controlled by the one driver at the front. Some BR diesel and electric locomotives can be coupled together and run *in multiple* with one driver controlling both from the front cab. Not all locomotive types are suitable for multiple working with other classes and need a driver on each.

The BR diesel multiple-unit (dmu) fleet eventually developed into three basic patterns respectively for suburban, general purpose and express Inter-City types. The suburban types can be identified by their side doors to each seating bay, and some have no toilets and no corridors between coaches; the general purpose units have two or three doors along the coach sides and usually have toilets and corridors within the unit, while the main line Inter-City sets have coaches which are similar in accommodation to locomotive-hauled stock of the late 1950s. They are used on principal cross-country routes where up to six-coach formations or so are adequate but something better than the general purpose units with their rather austere bus-type seating is required. Some of the suburban type units are single cars designed for branch duties on the few surviving branches.

In contrast in 1960 BR built several luxury diesel multiple-unit Pullman sets, some for the Midland route between London and Manchester being first class only, and others for the Western Region for London, Bristol and Birmingham business workings with first and second class. They featured full air-conditioning, meals at every seat, and in decor and materials were representative of the best in industrial design of the time. Clearly they were inspired by the luxury Trans Europ Express trains then gradually being introduced for selected international services linking European capitals and other major centres. Certainly the diesel Pullman units were far superior in riding and quietness to anything else on BR at that time. Since then BR engineers have been striving to achieve these standards for ordinary trains and new Inter-City coaches built during the last five years or so have included improved sound insulation, better riding, and full air conditioning for ordinary non-supplement services, one of the few railway administrations in the world to provide air-conditioning on ordinary everyday trains.

SOUTHERN ELECTRICS

On the Southern Region BR continued the policy of the former Southern Railway by extending the 660/750V dc third rail electrification system to nearly all lines east of the Basingstoke-Southampton route. The only exceptions are a few branch and cross-country routes where diesel multiple-units are used. In order to maintain standardised components as far as possible the Southern has its own brand of diesel train with electric transmission so that it can use the same electrical components as on its electric trains. Because the diesel generators providing electric power are too large to go under coach floors they are mounted in a compartment at one end of motor coaches. Apart from normal diesel-electric locomotives which the Southern uses for parcels and freight and a few passenger services, the Region has also developed a unique type of locomotive, the electro-diesel which can work as an ordinary electric locomotive taking current from the third rail of electrified lines, but with a small diesel generator can work as a diesel-electric locomotive on non-electrified lines.

Another feature pioneered by the Southern is push-pull working at express speeds. Short one or two coach push-pull trains were a feature of steam branches for many years but the Southern uses the principle on Waterloo-Bournemouth/Weymouth express trains at speeds of up to 90mph. Because the Bournemouth-Weymouth line is not electrified diesel locomotives are used to work passenger trains on this section, but the line is electrified between London and Bournemouth. To save working Weymouth trains under diesel power all the way from London or having electric multiple-units (emus) hauled dead by diesel locomotives on the non-electrified section the Southern compromised with a unique scheme of haulage. The Bournemouth line fast trains are formed in four-coach units, and the four including the restaurant car which are always detached at Bournemouth include two high horse-power electric motor coaches, together capable of giving out 3200hp. The other four-coach units are unpowered but like the four-coach powered units all have driving cabs at each end. The normal formation leaving London is two unpowered four-coach sets at the front with a four-coach electric high horse-power four-coach set at the back pushing the other eight coaches. These same unpowered four-coach sets can work in conjunction as up to 12 coach formations with diesel or electro-diesel locomotives at the front, back or intermediately between two sets.

NEW TYPES OF FREIGHT

Freight services have been revolutionised with new types of train including the container Freightliner services both for general traffic and for specific customers. Block trains, that is services in which a complete train of one product for one customer runs through from start to destination without intermediate remarshalling, are a common feature of today's freight services, particularly for oil, chemicals, cement, car components and car deliveries. Moreover most of today's freight trains have continuous automatic brakes throughout and do not need a guard's van at the back, and the guard rides on the locomotive.

TOMORROW'S TRAINS

For the future BR is aiming at higher speeds on existing track, first to 125mph with the High Speed Train (HST) — diesel-powered trains with locomotives (looking almost like a coach) at both ends and which will enter general service on the Western and Eastern Regions during 1976/77. Then comes the Advanced Passenger Train (APT), in which aircraft principles for body construction, and many innovations including body tilting to give passengers a comfortable ride when curves are taken at higher speeds than today, have been embodied to give a train of light construction so that ultra high-power will not be needed to attain speeds of up to 150mph, although far more power will be necessary than conventional trains of today. The type of construction, suspension and braking will allow the APT to travel at higher speeds on existing track and to take curves faster than conventional trains. In this way 150mph becomes a practical possibility without the impossibly high expenditure on a purpose-built railway as has been done in Japan.

Already 151mph has been achieved with the prototype gas turbine powered unit, on trials between Swindon and Reading during August 1975 but the first production units are expected to be electrically-powered for the West Coast main line and could provide times as short as 4 hours between London and Glasgow by the 1980s.

This book looks at the modernised British Rail, the system we know today, mostly at the locomotives and trains in action, but also the ancillary features which go to make up the complete railway. In compiling the photographs I must acknowledge with thanks the assistance of all the photographers who are individually credited.

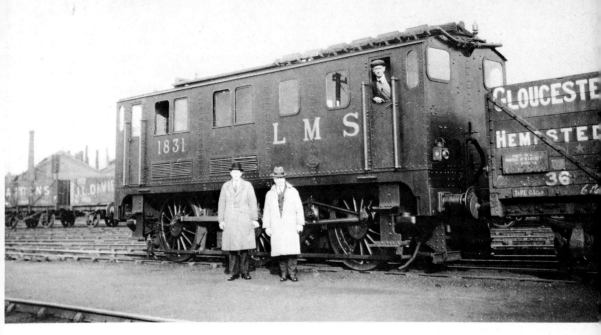

1 THE PIONEERS

Above: The LMS was the pioneer British railway company to make use of diesel locomotives for shunting purposes. In 1932 it built an experimental 0-6-0 diesel hydraulic locomotive by using the chassis of an old Midland Railway 0-6-0 steam tank engine and mounting on it a 400hp Davey-Paxman diesel engine coupled to hydraulic transmission. The locomotive, numbered 1831, was used during the 1930s and was followed by various types of diesel shunter, although eventually electric transmission was standardised. *Locomotive & General Railway Photographs*

Below: One of the more unusual LMS experiments of the 1930s was this Karrier bus equipped with road and rail wheels intended to work over railway lines as far as a suitable change-over point where it could take the road to serve villages not immediately close to the railway. It was used on the Blisworth-Towcester-Stratford-on-Avon line. *Locomotive & General Railway Photographs*

Above: During the 1930s the Great Western Railway pioneered the use of diesel railcars for passenger services on branches and for local duties on main lines. Several batches were built before and during the second world war and much valuable experience was gained from them when the British Railways fleet of diesel multiple-unit trains was being designed in the mid-1950s. These GWR railcars introduced the two-tone warning horn so familiar today on BR.
Locomotive & General Railway Photographs

Left: So popular were the GWR railcars that the company built some for longer distance cross-country services, including buffet facilities.
British Railways

Above: Just before nationalisation the LMS had planned the introduction of main line diesel locomotive prototypes of which the first was No 10000, a 1600hp machine built by English Electric. With its sister, No 10001, it worked on local and express services on various parts of the London Midland Region and later Southern Region. It is seen here passing Kenton with a Bletchley-Euston local in September 1959.

Derek Cross

Above: The Southern Railway also planned the introduction of main line diesel locomotives after the second world war and three were completed in 1951/54 of which No 10203 of 2000hp was the most powerful. Like the LMS locomotives it was built by English Electric but had the unusual wheel arrangement of 1Co-Co1 and later formed the general prototype for the English Electric Class 40 developed during the mid-1950s. No 10203 is seen here at Shap summit cutting with the up Royal Scot from Glasgow to Euston on 1 August 1958. *Derek Cross*

Below: Another of the Southern diesel-electrics, No 10201 of 1750hp, also seen at work on the LMR with the 16.15 Euston-Bletchley near Kenton in the late 1950s. *G M Kichenside*

Above: The Great Western was also looking into the question of internal combustion traction at the time of nationalisation but in the form of a gas-turbine power plant. The first locomotive, No 18000, was ordered from the Swiss firm Brown-Boveri and delivered in 1949. It is seen here six years later near Didcot with a Bristol-Paddington train. Later the locomotive was returned to Switzerland and today is used as a research vehicle by the International Union of Railways Research Section.

T E Williams

Below: The second gas-turbine locomotive built for the WR was No 18100 constructed by Metropolitan-Vickers and completed in 1951. Both the gas-turbine locomotives employed electric transmission in which the gas-turbine powered a generator. This locomotive was later re-equipped as the prototype 25,000V ac electric locomotive for which it was fitted with a pantograph, for experimental work in connection with main line electrification between Manchester and London. It is seen here in its original condition at Paddington with a down Bristol train on 31 May 1952.

Stanley Creer

2 ELECTRICS INHERITED—NER AND LMR

Above: Electric traction is by no means new and one or two main line companies converted some suburban lines to electric working soon after the turn of the century. This is one of the motor coaches built by the North Eastern Railway to inaugurate its 1903 Tyneside electrification, but withdrawn after a carriage shed fire in 1918. *Locomotive & General Railway Photographs*

Top right: An early 1960s view of a North Tyneside electric train crossing the East Coast main line near Forest Hall. These trains, built by the LNER in 1937, were formed into pairs of articulated coaches. When they were life expired in 1967 the Tyneside routes were de-electrified and diesel trains took over. However, some of these lines are to be re-electrified as part of the Tyneside rapid transit line now being built through the heart of Newcastle. *I S Carr*

Bottom right: British Railways built some two-car electric trains similar in style to those for the Southern Region, for South Tyneside lines in Newcastle. A six-car train is seen on the High-Level bridge heading for Gateshead and South Shields. When electric services in Newcastle finished in 1967 these trains were transferred to the Southern Region. *Kenneth Field*

Above: During the early 1930s the future standard system of electrification was planned to be 1500V dc with overhead collection. The first line to be converted to this system was that between Manchester and Altrincham for which new trains, basically of LMS type compartment stock, were built. This line was jointly worked by the LMS and LNER but in recent years became part of the London Midland Region and a few years ago was converted to 25000V ac to form an end-on connection with the existing Manchester-Crewe electrified line.

Locomotive & General Railway Photographs

Below: Another pioneer electric line was the Midland branch between Lancaster, Morecambe and Heysham which employed 25 cycle (Hz) alternating current at 6600V. During the mid-1950s the electrical supply was converted to 6250V at 50Hz industrial frequency and some old London-area electric trains were adapted to work on the new system as a prototype for the future standard high voltage alternating current system on BR.

British Railways

Above: The Lancashire & Yorkshire Railway also went for electrification on two of its Liverpool and Manchester suburban lines. The Manchester-Bury line used 1200V dc but employed a protected side-contact third rail for current collection. Although these original trains have long since been withdrawn and replaced by British Railways type coaches, plans are in hand for conversion of this line to the high voltage alternating current system.

Locomotive & General Railway Photographs

Below: The Mersey Railway linking Liverpool and Birkenhead was also a pioneer of electrification when the route through the Mersey tunnel was electrified in 1904. In 1938 the LMS electrified its related route to West Kirby and provided new trains with sliding doors and open saloon interiors to work the service. These coaches were of lightweight construction and were slightly smaller in profile than conventional main line coaches. BR built some more in 1956 to replace the original Mersey Railway trains.

British Railways

Above: When the LMS built new trains for the Liverpool-Southport line in 1939/40 again it adopted sliding doors with a saloon layout but the Southport line coaches were among the longest ever built in this country at 66ft and were slightly wider than normal main line stock.

Below: The Southport line stock of 1939 included five-aside seating with two seats on one side of the passageway and three on the other, and despite the use of sliding doors which has been held in some quarters to cut down seating capacity, the second class trailer cars seat no fewer than 102 passengers. The two-plus-three seating arrangement has been adopted widely by British Railways on most suburban diesel and electric stock but usually with side swing doors.

British Railways

Above: The London & North Western also went in for electrification on its Euston-Watford and Broad Street-Richmond suburban lines between 1915 and 1922. The three-coach trains, of which one is seen here leaving Euston, had end hand-operated sliding doors, and seating comfort quite the equal of any main line stock. They were withdrawn in the late 1950s.

G M Kichenside

Right: To replace the former LNWR electric trains British Railways built a series of three-coach units with side swing doors and both compartment and open saloon layout, These trains are still in service today. *Rev G B Wise*

Below: During the late 1920s the LMS augmented the stock for the Euston and Broad Street suburban lines with compartment-type trains very similar to ordinary LMS steam-hauled suburban coaches. *British Railways*

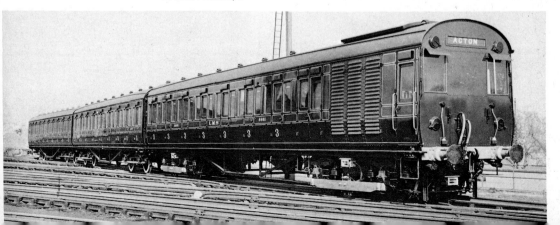

3 ELECTRICS INHERITED—THE SOUTHERN

During the 1920s and 1930s the Southern Railway, in undertaking extensions to its electrified suburban network provided new electric trains by converting and rebuilding existing steam-hauled coaches, no more than ten and in a few cases 20 years old. With restrictions on capital expenditure after the second world war the result was that some of these electric trains lasted into the late 1950s by which time the coach bodies and their somewhat spartan accommodation were well over 40 years old. Moreover, as the underframes and mechanical equipment were only about 20 years old the Southern Region re-used the underframes with new bodies to form the replacement stock in the early 1960s. *Top left* is a former London, Brighton & South Coast type unit seen at Hampton Court in 1957 and, *bottom left,* part of a two-coach unit which worked the Waterloo-Windsor/Weybridge service until 1957. *Above:* The Southern Railway built two batches of new suburban electric trains in 1925, one type for services from Charing Cross, the other illustrated here for services from Waterloo. Originally they were made up as three-car trains but after the second world war extra coaches were inserted to form four-coach trains.

G M Kichenside

Above: A train of two-car suburban electric units built in the late 1950s to modern Southern style but utilising the underframes of the old wooden-bodied coaches seen bottom left on the previous page. *G M Kichenside*

Below: The standard post-war Southern Railway four-coach suburban train is still used all over the Southern Region on London area services. They can be distinguished by their rounded windows and independent top-light windows in the doors. An eight-coach train of this stock crosses Richmond Bridge on 30 January 1965. *G M Kichenside*

Above: Southern Railway electric stock was classified broadly into three types—suburban, semi-fast, and express. The semi-fast units consisted of a number of sub-types but most were of compartment pattern, some with side corridors and toilets in one or both coaches. This two-coach semi-fast unit No 2016, classified by the SR as 2BIL, forms part of a six-coach train between Portsmouth and Brighton and was photographed at Havant in September 1964.

G M Kichenside

Below: The four-coach semi-fast trains provided for the London-Brighton line in 1932 included one coach with a corridor and toilets and while the others were of the non-corridor compartment pattern the third class compartments included arm-rests to divide the seating into two-one-two so that passengers had main line standards of comfort. Unit No 2932 waits to leave Brighton for Victoria in the mid 1950s

Kenneth Field

Even though the longest Southern Electric main line journeys from London to South Coast resorts occupied no more than one to two hours the Southern provided trains quite the equal of long-distance corridor stock on other lines, and on its Brighton line services even included Pullman cars with meals and refreshments at your seat on most services. *Top left* is one of the six-coach corridor units, including a Pullman car, used between London, Brighton, Littlehampton and Hastings; *bottom left* is a close-up of one of the Pullman cars, *Enid,* which included first and third class accommodation and a kitchen. *Above:* Pullman cars did not feature on the Portsmouth main line and the 12-car express trains formed of three four-car units coupled together included full restaurant facilities usually in the middle unit. An up Portsmouth express is seen approaching Raynes Park on 4 August 1962.   *G M Kichenside*

4 BR DIESEL LOCOMOTIVES

Above: One of the disappointing classes was the English Electric type 2 using a single Deltic type power plant, particularly compared with its brilliant bigger sisters of 3300hp employed so successfully on East Coast expresses. Here No D5902 heads past Brookmans Park with a Cambridge-Kings Cross outer suburban train in July 1960. *Derek Cross*

Top left: Originally British Railways ordered three classes of type 1 diesel locomotive for short distance freight and passenger working, of which this is an example of the second type, built by BTH. No D8231 heads an empty stock train from Hornsey to Kings Cross in the early 1960s. *Kenneth Field*

Left: The only surviving type 1 locomotive, now known as Class 20, is that built by the English Electric Co and totalling over 200 examples. No D8013 passes Camden Road Junction on the North London line with a freight from the Eastern Region to Willesden in the late 1950s. *Kenneth Field*

Left: The Scottish Region provided new standards of service between Glasgow and Edinburgh to replace older dmu trains in the early 1970s by adapting modern locomotive-hauled coaches displaced from other lines by later deliveries with through control cables and new braking equipment for working with diesel locomotives at both ends at the same time, controlled by the driver in the leading cab. This provided not only sufficient power for a high-speed service but avoided locomotive movements at terminals. The motive power is provided by pairs of 1250hp class 27 locomotives, originally BR type 2, built by the Birmingham RCW Co. Nos 27 115/8 work the 17.00 Glasgow-Edinburgh through Falkirk on 23 June 1974. *D Griffiths*

Bottom left: The Scottish Region makes extensive use of type 2 motive power on the Highland lines, either singly or in pairs. Nos 5315 and 5065 stand on the left with an Inverness-Edinburgh train waiting to pass Nos 5129 and 5341 on the 14.40 Edinburgh-Inverness at Dalwhinnie on 9 July 1971 in the heart of the Scottish Highland mountains. *D Griffiths*

Below: A Birmingham RCW type 2 diesel heads the 10.38 Inverness-Kyle of Lochalsh over the stark open moorland near Achnasheen on 6 July 1973. *John Goss*

Above: Class 25 No 5203 heads a van train towards Sheffield at Chinley on 27 October 1973.

C Plant

Below: Another class 25, this time No 5173, works a freight down the East Coast main line at Newton Hall north of Durham on 15 April 1965. Because of the limited brake power of diesel locomotives when working freight trains without continuous automatic brakes, brake tenders are attached to some diesel locomotives to provide additional brake force to assist in controlling loose-coupled freight trains. Here the brake tender can be seen between the locomotive and first wagon.

I S Carr

Above: For a time during the late 1950s to allow the withdrawal of ageing steam locomotives a number of diesel locomotives ultimately intended for the London Midland Region were loaned to the Southern Region which employed them on local passenger services in Kent pending electrification. Here type 2 (now class 25) No 5017 passes Bearsted with a Maidstone East-Ashford train on 23 April 1960.

Stanley Creer

Below: The Western Region developed the type 2 version in diesel-hydraulic form for branch and local services; No D6353, one of the North British built locomotives, stands at Helston after arriving with the 10.55 from Gwinear Road on 20 August 1962, a branch now but a memory.

C S Heaps

Above: One of the earliest of the BR type 2 locomotives built by Brush Traction Co was originally allocated to the Eastern Region. They were unusual in having six-wheel bogies with one unpowered axle in each. Now known as Class 31 some members of the class have been transferred to the Western Region to replace withdrawn diesel-hydraulic locomotives. Here No 31 412 leaves Taunton with a Paddington-Barnstaple summer Saturday express in July 1974.

K Connolly

Top left: Another class 31 still with its original number 5808 heads an Eastern Region bridge inspection unit at Bawtry on the East Coast main line. The area here has been liable to mining subsidence which has resulted in strengthening work being undertaken on the viaduct to overcome the speed restriction previously needed.

C Plant

Bottom left: Class 31 No 5528 based at Old Oak Common depot heads a freight train near Pangbourne on 26 April 1973. In common with many classes built in the early days of the diesel programme this one is fitted with headcode discs to indicate the train classification rather than the later alpha-numerical indicators.

G F Gillham

Above: Intermediate in the power range of the BR diesel fleet is the English Electric type 3 of 1750hp, now known as class 37. No 6801 heads an up mixed freight between Selby and Doncaster in June 1973.   *G T Heavyside*

Top left: The Western Region developed its own brand of type 3 locomotive in hydraulic form with a class built by Beyer-Peacock, a firm noted for many years for its articulated steam locomotives of the Garratt type. The Beyer-Peacock Type 3s, also known as Hymeks and later as class 35, performed useful work on secondary express duties but all have now been withdrawn. No D7018 heads a Bristol-Paddington express at Box on 16 April 1963.   *G A Richardson*

Bottom left: Sister locomotive No D7074 takes a westbound freight for Exeter past Blatchbridge Junction at the west end of the Frome loop on 8 June 1964.   *Derek Cross*

Above: Another Class 37 in action, this time No 6734 seen here soon after leaving Cowtown Tunnel on the Hope Valley route between Manchester and Sheffield with the 14.40 Manchester Piccadilly-Harwich boat train on 26 April 1973. This working continues a long steam tradition in which engines from East Anglian sheds worked through to Sheffield, York or Manchester with the North Country Continental boat train.   *C Plant*

Top right: The Southern also has its own brand of type 3 locomotive, now known as class 33, which are equally at home on passenger or freight working. Although all are based on the Southern Region, largely because their control system is unique in that it can inter-work in multiple with Southern electro-diesel locomotives and electric multiple-unit trains, some duties take these locomotives over other regions on through workings. For a time one of them worked up the East Coast main line to York and beyond with a block load of cement wagons from North Kent to Scotland. Here No D6575 returns with the empties near Grantham on 18 May 1963.
John K Morton

Bottom right: Another through working with SR Class 33s takes them on to the Western Region with the Waterloo-Exeter passenger trains and sometimes they are used on fill-in duties beyond Exeter to Plymouth. Here an unidentified Class 33 climbs away from Honiton with the 10.10 Exeter St Davids-Waterloo on 14 April 1974.

P J Fowler

Above: One of the first of the modernisation plan diesels for express passenger workings was the English Electric type 4 in the D200 series introduced in 1958 and now known as Class 40. Their first duties found them on Liverpool Street-Norwich trains and services from Euston and Kings Cross. Here No D296 arrives at Manchester Piccadilly with an express from Euston in the early 1960s after electric working had been inaugurated between Manchester and Crewe. *Kenneth Field*

Above: Although not so often used on top line express passenger working now because higher power units of other classes have replaced them, the English Electric Class 40s still find employment on widespread duties including freight workings. Class 40 No 204 passes the site of Peak Forest Station on the former Midland main line with a freight on 22 September 1973. *C Plant*

Left: In the transition period from steam to diesel, diesel locomotives often found themselves working with steam to provide additional power as here where English Electric type 4 No D292 pilots Stanier Class 5 4-6-0 No 45161 with a 16-coach Glasgow-Birmingham train in July 1962.

Derek Cross

Above: Slightly more powerful than its English Electric counterpart is the British Railways built type 4 now known as Classes 44, 45, 46 with power in the range 2300 to 2500hp. These locomotives are equally used widely on passenger and freight services and, moreover, can be found in many parts of the country because of their use on cross-country routes. An unidentified Class 45/6 heads down the Midland main line with an express from St Pancras near Mill Hill where the route runs parallel with the M1 motorway.

Right: The important north and west Inter-City passenger service is largely in the hands of Class 45/6 locomotives and here No 140 approaches the outskirts of Bristol with the 07.40 Penzance-Liverpool Lime Street on 26 November 1973.   *P J Fowler*

Below: Class 45 No 137 *The Cheshire Regiment* heads a bulk cement train towards Manchester through Chinley in October 1973.   *C Plant*

Above: Some of the duties carried out by the BR Class 45/6 locomotives take them right across the country from the North East to the far South West on such workings as Newcastle or Leeds to Plymouth or Penzance. Class 46 No 165 draws to a halt at Newcastle with the 16.15 to Bristol on 28 August 1972.
G T Heavyside

Above: First of the WR type 4 diesel-hydraulics were a batch of five built by the North British Locomotive Co and numbered D600 to D604. All were named after warships, although they were totally dissimilar to the later and principal batch of Warship class locomotives built by Swindon and North British Locomotive Co a year or two later. The first of the class No D600 *Active* slows for bridge rebuilding at West Drayton with the down Cornish Riviera Express in February 1960.

C R L Coles

Left: Quite a number of the Class 44, 45 and 46 locomotives carry names, the first ten of Class 44 named after Peaks in the Pennines, Lake District and North Wales and which have given the name Peak to the entire class. All the other locomotives of the class which are named have taken the titles of army regiments, many of which were carried by Royal Scot steam locomotives on the LMS. This is a close-up of *The Staffordshire Regiment (the Prince of Wales's),* locomotive No D71.

C Plant

Left: One of the North British Locomotive Co's main batch of Warship Class locomotives, following very much German practice in appearance and equipment, No D834 *Pathfinder,* leaves the western portal of Box Tunnel with the Bristol Pullman on 16 April 1963. This was a substitute train for the air-conditioned diesel multiple-unit Blue Pullman unit which normally provided this service.   *G A Richardson*

Bottom left: All the WR diesel-hydraulic classes with the exception of the Westerns—also known as class 52—have now been withdrawn but as these notes are written the Western class is gradually disappearing. For over a decade they were the mainstay of principal Western Region express passenger services, particularly on the West of England line. Here No 1029 *Western Legionnaire* winds round the curves near Burngullow with the 11.10 Penzance-Manchester Piccadilly on 23 June 1973.   *C Plant*

Below: Although used on express passenger work the Western class locomotives were equally at home on freight and particularly on the stone trains from Merehead quarry near Witham on the West of England main line. No 1015 *Western Champion* approaches Fairwood Junction from the Westbury Loop with empty wagons for Merehead on 4 June 1974.   *K Connolly*

Above: The Brush Traction Co built type 4 of class 47, equipped with Sulzer engines, can be found on most regions of British Railways and on the Western Region is gradually taking over workings by the Western class 52s. Here No 1642 wades out of Newbury after heavy rain with the 9.30 Paddington-Paignton on 11 June 1971. *D E Canning*

Right: With much of the overhead catenary in position for the GN line suburban electrification to Hitchin and Royston Brush class 47 No 47 542 speeds through the tunnels near Hadley Wood with the 7.20 from Newcastle to Kings Cross on 24 May 1975. *Kevin Lane*

More examples of the widespread use of Brush class 47s on express passenger work: *left,*
No D1709 heads the 16.10 Paddington-Wolverhampton near Gerrards Cross on 16 May 1964
during the time the GW route to Birmingham carried all traffic from London while the LMR route
was electrified. *Bottom left:* No 1554 stands at Perth with a Motorail service on 19 August 1972.
Below: No 1921 waits at Exeter St Davids with the down Cornish Riviera Express on 3 April 1969.
C R L Coles; D Griffiths; G F Gillham

Above: The English Electric class 50s were the last express passenger diesel locomotive type to be built, in 1967. They were originally intended for use in pairs between Crewe and Glasgow while the northern end of the West Coast main line was electrified and now most of them have been displaced from these duties and some transferred to the Western Region. These locomotives, together with the Deltics on the East Coast main line, are the only diesels on BR apart from the HST officially passed to run at 100mph although some of the other types with maxima of 90 or 95mph occasionally touch 100mph. Here a pair of class 50s work the up Royal Scot from Glasgow to Euston through the Lune Gorge just south of Tebay alongside the M6 motorway which closely follows the railway in this area. The date is 1973. *M Dunnett*

Right: Class 50 No 50 023 speeds out of the east end of Box Tunnel with a train of air-conditioned stock forming the 11.40 Weston-super-Mare—Paddington on 22 June 1974 *P J Fowler*

Below: Class 50 No 447 arrives at Crewe from the north with an up parcels train on 15 July 1972. *C Plant*

Left: Currently the most powerful type of diesel locomotives on British Railways, the 3300hp Deltic, originally numbered in the D9000 series and now known as class 55. Here No 9010 *The King's Own Scottish Borderer* waits to leave Kings Cross with the Flying Scotsman in the early 1960s. *Kenneth Field*

Bottom left: Still carrying it old number class 55 No 9006 *The Fife and Forfar Yeomanry* passes Doncaster with a Kings Cross-Edinburgh express on 29 May 1972. *G T Heavyside*

Below: Today's standard BR diesel electric shunter, a successor to those LMS experiments of 40 years ago. *C Plant*

Above: During the 1960s British Railways provided test running facilities for a number of prototype locomotives built by individual locomotive manufacturers to try out new ideas and to act as a shop window for British Railways and other railway administrations in the hope of attracting production orders. This is No D 0260 *Lion* sometimes known as the *White Lion* because of its all-white livery built by the Birmingham RCW Co in 1962. It is seen at Paddington on 17 May of that year waiting to work the 12.10 to Birmingham. This particular design was not proceeded with and the locomotive was taken out of traffic after a few years.   *Rev G B Wise*

Below: The prototype Brush Type 4, originally No D 0280 but later renumbered 1200 *Falcon*, equipped with two high speed diesel engines similar to those of the diesel-hydraulic class 52s, but employed with electric transmission. Here No 1200 heads the 18.40 Fridays only Paddington— Weston-super-Mare on 16 June 1972. This is the only one of the diesel prototypes left in service.   *G F Gillham*

Above: The original English Electric *Deltic* locomotive, constructed to demonstrate the potential of the Napier Deltic diesel engine originally produced for marine use and to show off a locomotive far more powerful than any other in the BR diesel fleet as originally envisaged, ran most of its trials on both the East Coast main line and on the West Coast services between Euston and Liverpool. It is seen here accelerating away from Crewe with an up Liverpool-Euston train on 7 July 1958. Eventually the Eastern Region ordered 22 locomotives of this type, while the prototype in its handsome blue and yellow livery has been preserved in the Science Museum, London.

R W Hinton

Below: Another of the prototypes, although very short-lived as far as BR was concerned, was the Hawker-Siddeley *Kestrel* of 4000hp and numbered HS 4000. In its attractive two-tone brown and cream livery it leaves Heaton carriage sidings with the empty stock to form the 16.45 Newcastle-Kings Cross on 28 October 1969. BR could not foresee a long-term future for a locomotive of this power and with re-gauged bogies it was later sold to Russia.

I S Carr

5 DIESEL MULTIPLE-UNITS

Above: During the late 1950s as part of the dieselisation programme BR looked at the possibility of using lightweight four-wheel diesel railbuses on branch lines with very light traffic. Most were designed to operate as single cars but a three-coach set was built by Associated Commercial Vehicles, part of the AEC/Leyland organisation, seen here on the Belmont branch in March 1959.

G M Kichenside

Below: One of the first areas to receive diesel multiple-unit (dmu) trains was Cumberland but unfortunately they could not stem losses and this unit is seen at Cockermouth on the 9.25 Workington-Penrith-Carlisle service on 2 April 1966 shortly before withdrawal of services between Workington and Keswick.

I S Carr

Above: A three-car dmu crosses the attractive viaduct over the river Nidd at Knaresborough on a working to Leeds. *Kenneth Field*

Below: Dmus were adopted widely in East Anglia during the 1950s but they still did not save certain services, as for example the Aldeburgh branch from Saxmundham photographed here on 23 June 1961. *S Creer*

In 1960 British Railways launched into the realms of the high-speed luxury train, fully air-conditioned and with accommodation quite the equal of the world's best in design and sound insulation for relatively short daytime journeys. These trains were formed into set units with a diesel-electric powered motor coach at each end and ran under the Pullman banner with meal service at every seat. The original units ran between St Pancras and Manchester, Paddington and Birmingham, and Paddington and Bristol but later all the units were concentrated on the Western Region. This is the Birmingham Pullman passing Gerrards Cross in July 1961.　　*C R L Coles*

Right: One of the 'tadpole' units of the Southern Region; these three-car trains with a diesel-electric motor coach at one end were compromise sets made up by the Southern Region economically from redundant diesel and electric stock from other lines. The former electric driving trailer at the far end with a 9ft wide body was adapted to work with the two diesel coaches of narrow-bodied Hastings-line stock which gives them this wide and narrow appearance and their nickname. They were designed for the Reading-Redhill-Tonbridge service but this unit is seen on a test run passing Thatcham on the Western Region Berks & Hants line early one Sunday morning in June 1973.　　*D E Canning*

Above: Some of the longer distance cross-country services were provided with dmus having similar accommodation to ordinary Inter-City locomotive-hauled coaches. Most dmus provide passengers with a view forward through the driver's cab, enhanced by these panoramic wrap-round windscreens featured in this Hull-Liverpool Trans-Pennine unit seen here at Slaithwaite viaduct. The wrap-round windows have more recently been abandoned on recent designs because of their vulnerability to vandals by stone throwing. *Kenneth Field*

Top left: The single diesel railcar of the Looe branch waits to leave Liskeard on 16 July 1969. This is one of the few branches in the South West retaining passenger services. *G F Gillham*

Bottom left: A typical suburban dmu with side doors to each seating bay and used on many commuter routes around London and elsewhere. Despite the fact that many of these trains have toilets in only one coach without access from the others, or even no toilet facilities at all, they are often used on longer-distance stopping services on main lines. *C R L Coles*

6 1500V DC ELECTRICS

One of the major electrification schemes inherited by BR was the LNER project for the conversion of the Manchester-Sheffield/Wath lines via the Woodhead route through the Pennines, which involved the boring of a new double track Woodhead tunnel to replace the original pair of single tunnels, unsuited to electrification. It employed 1500 volts direct current and was commissioned in 1954. Through passenger services by this route were later withdrawn and today the line is used for heavy freight including coal with a merry-go-round load seen here double-headed by locomotives 76 025 and 76 007.   *Barry J Nicolle*

7 GREAT EASTERN ELECTRIC

Another LNER electrification scheme completed by BR was that between Liverpool Street and Shenfield in 1949. The system was later extended to Southend and Chelmsford and in 1960 was converted to high voltage alternating current for further extensions to Clacton and Bishops Stortford. Here one of the original trains of 1949, with sliding doors and open saloon interiors and seen after conversion for ac working which involved rebuilding motor and trailer coaches to take new electrical equipment, is seen approaching Ingatestone in May 1971. *G R Mortimer*

Above: The Clacton and Walton branches were used for trials with high voltage alternating current traction with the first electric trains delivered to the area in the late 1950s. When through electric working to London could be started in 1962, Clacton/Walton-Liverpool Street expresses were formed of new main line stock capable of 100mph running on suitable lengths of track. Like contemporary electric stock in the Glasgow area they had the wrap-round windscreens, but passengers were not given the view through the driver's cab as in diesel trains. The trains are formed into two- and four-coach units. A Clacton express is seen here passing Alresford in August 1970. *G R Mortimer*

As part of the Great Eastern area electrification schemes both routes to Southend from Liverpool Street and Fenchurch Street were electrified. *Top left* is a train of earlier BR outer suburban ac stock leaving Chalkwell for Shoeburyness and *bottom left,* a train of later stock with sloped back front-end passing Stratford on a working into Liverpool Street. *G M Kichenside*

8 WEST COAST ELECTRICS

Above: A typical West Coast Inter-City electric of today with one of the latest electric locomotives No 87 024 leaving Linsdale Tunnel in August 1974 with a train of air-conditioned Mark II stock forming a down express. This class of locomotive was the first to be built without a headcode panel following the decision to abandon the display of train headcodes on new stock, since with centralised power signalling the trains themselves are rarely seen by the signalmen in modern power signalboxes. The train number though would have been useful for platform staff to identify particular trains. Instead BR is returning to headlights to mark the front of trains, only to give warning of approach and not as a code to denote class of train. *British Railways*

Top left: Soon after the commissioning of electric working between Manchester Piccadilly and Crewe in 1960 an unidentified Class 83 locomotive leaves Piccadilly with a train for the Western Region. *Kenneth Field*

Bottom left: In the days when stationmasters at principal stations still wore top hats, and interest in new locomotives by the platform end observers was as great as ever. A special demonstration trip by one of the first of the new West Coast electrics stands at Crewe waiting to leave for Manchester in 1960. *Kenneth Field*

Top left: The first of the electric multiple-units (emus) for high-voltage ac services looked little different from normal BR suburban stock with side doors to each compartment or seating bay. Some attempt however was made to produce a feature front end with a slope back to the windows and domed roof front, instead of the normal square slab front which had characterised British electric trains for half a century. This unit is seen at the Altrincham line platforms at Manchester Piccadilly waiting to leave for Crewe, although it was to be another decade in the early 70s before ac electric trains eventually reached Altrincham. *Kenneth Field*

Bottom left: By the time the southern end of the West Coast main line into Euston was electrified BR designers had evolved the attractive front end with swept round windscreens for the Glasgow and Clacton electric services and adopted it for the semi-fast outer suburban electric trains working to and from Euston. These four-car units also featured integral body design in which the body and chassis were constructed as one stress-bearing unit and in order to gain strength certain seating bays did not have external doors. These units also have electro-pneumatically-operated disc brakes, and like all other recently constructed emus include only one power car in the middle, with driving trailer cars at each end. Similar types of unit are in course of delivery for Kings Cross-Royston outer suburban services, although the wrap-round windscreen has been abandoned for a flat front window which can more easily be made of toughened glass to withstand impacts with birds or other objects. *British Railways*

Below: The majority of through freight services on the West Coast main line are also electrically-hauled and so too are car delivery trains such as this one seen passing Watford Junction bound for Willesden and the Eastern Region in October 1965, a month or so before the catenary into Euston was energised. *C R L Coles*

The northern end of the electrified West Coast main line which was finally linked to the London end of the system in May 1974. Class 86 042 leaves Glasgow Central with the 17.45 to Birmingham, named The Midland Scot, on 23 May 1974.   *G T Heavyside*

9 THE SOUTHERN IN THE SEVENTIES

Above: During the 1960s the Southern developed new trains for its London to Brighton and Portsmouth services which by this time were firmly in the realms of the commuter belt and with a traffic far more outer suburban in character than main line Inter-City. The new trains were broadly based on standard Inter-City type stock of the previous decade or so but included extra doors without loss of seating capacity to suit the commuter nature of the services. Southern electric stock has always been classified by a figure denoting the number of coaches in a set together with a three-letter code giving some indication of the type of accommodation provided. These units are known as 4CIG (or 4BIG if they include a buffet car) the IG part of the code being the old telegraphic code for Brighton. A 12-car train of 4CIG/BIG stock passes Merstham on the Quarry Line on a Victoria-Littlehampton working in May 1972. *Stanley Creer*

Top right: For the Bournemouth electrification in 1967 the Southern adopted a system of push-pull working with a four-car powered unit at the Waterloo end pushing two unpowered four-car units at the leading end, but with the driver controlling the train from the front. This system was to allow diesel working of the front unit from Bournemouth to Weymouth, which is not electrified. A 12-car Bournemouth and Weymouth train is seen here passing Surbiton with the unpowered units at the front. *G M Kichenside*

Bottom right: The same train seen from the back with the powered unit No 3011 propelling the front eight cars as it passes Surbiton. *G M Kichenside*

74

Above: History in the making. The first electrically-worked Golden Arrow boat train between Victoria and Dover seen here passing Beckenham Junction headed by newly-built electric locomotive No E5015 in 1961. With luxury traffic eaten away by air competition and by private motoring, the need for services such as this diminished and the train was withdrawn in October 1972.

Stanley Creer

Above: The Brighton line had almost 90 years of unbroken Pullman tradition dating from the 1880s when the first Pullman cars providing luxury unknown on ordinary British trains at that time were introduced to the route. For a few pence extra on the ordinary fare passengers could have the luxury of individual service of refreshments at their seats and standards of heating and lighting way above those of other mid-Victorian trains. From the late 1880s a train of Pullman cars only operated on selected services and lasted into Southern Railway days, by which time from 1933 the first all-electric Pullman in the world had replaced the earlier steam-hauled train. The Brighton Belle, as it was now known, lasted for just under 40 years and made its last run in April 1972 when British Railways decided that the individuality of Pullman service was no longer an essential feature of what is basically a commuter line. Many of the Belle coaches have been preserved individually as restaurants in different parts of the country. *Stanley Creer*

Above: In contrast to the luxury illustrated on the previous two pages other Southern routes were not so fortunate and commuter services into Waterloo from the outer South Western suburbs are maintained by the rather spartan two and four coach units, some with through corridors and others without, illustrated here passing Surbiton on an Alton-Waterloo working in the early 1970s.

G M Kichenside

10 THE FREIGHT REVOLUTION

Below: The last ten years or so have seen a considerable change in freight train operation on British Railways. Although trains of individual wagons, each carrying different loads for different destinations and requiring re-marshalling en route, have not entirely disappeared, the emphasis has been on single train loads of one commodity to one destination. Among the new types of train are block loads for individual companies carrying their products alone and in particular such things as oil, cement, aggregates and other bulk commodities, which lend themselves readily to rail transport. A Class 52 locomotive draws slowly into Thatcham station waiting for signals to clear with a block load of stone from Foster Yeoman quarries at Merehead near Frome which are despatched to various parts of the country. A fleet of wagons has been built specially for this traffic and incorporates modern type suspension and air-operated disc brakes to allow running at much higher speeds than the 45mph permitted to ordinary wagons.　　　　*D E Canning*

Above: For general freight BR developed the Freightliner container system during the 1960s with road collection and delivery at the extremities of the journey with rail used for trunk haulage in the middle. The Freightliner company itself provides many of the containers but some companies with enough regular traffic have their own privately-owned containers in their own liveries and fleet name. An up Freightliner train approaches Linsdale Tunnel just north of Leighton Buzzard in August 1974.

British Railways

Below: Another block load, this time of cement wagons, is seen here near Edale behind English Electric class 40 No 230 heading for the nearby Hope Sidings for re-loading at the cement company's works on 31 August 1972.   *C Plant*

Above: One of the largest of the new BR freight wagon types is the 100-ton tank wagon built for oil, chemicals, etc. With a quarter of the total weight taken up by the wagon itself, about 75% of the gross permissible weight is allowed for the payload. Here Class 87 032 heads up the West Coast main line near Leighton Buzzard with a full load of chemical products from Merseyside to the British Oxygen Co siding at North Wembley in August 1974. *British Railways*

Top left: Another new type of freight service known as merry-go-round which involves hopper wagons, takes bulk loads of certain types of freight particularly coal, right into factory or power station sites where the material is unloaded while the train is on the move at dead slow speed. With similar loading facilities at the starting station the train theoretically is always on the move. Merry-go-round is also used, as illustrated here, for the supply of gypsum to a modern cement works in Kent, where class 33 No 6594 is seen at the head of the hopper wagons.

British Railways

Left: Another type of wagon used for carrying cars on delivery from manufacturers is the double-deck articulated type known as Cartic-4 marshalled into four-wagon units. Cars are thus transported from the major car-assembly factories to distribution centres around the country and to ports for export. *British Railways*

Right: The short-wheelbase four-wheel traditional British wagon soon showed that it was unsuitable for running at the higher speeds of the diesel and electric age and trains including the old type wagons are now restricted to 45mph. Wagon defects such as hot axleboxes can also lead to derailment as here at Hungerford in 1972 which caused extensive damage to the train and wrecked the signalbox.

D E Canning

11 SERVICING THE FLEET

Above: For the diesel age new depots had to be constructed to ensure ease of maintenance and access to the interior of locomotives. Many depots have this multi-stage arrangement of a pit and a high level walkway, allowing fitters to get at the underside of locomotives and into the body. Most of the Western Region diesel-hydraulics were maintained on the repair-by-replacement system in which components needing servicing were exchanged with ones freshly overhauled.
C Plant

Left: Some depots undertaking major maintenance are equipped with jacks for lifting locomotive bodies off bogies and with overhead cranes for removing the heavy diesel-electric generator sets. Here fitters tackle a job underneath class 45 No D123 at Toton depot. *British Railways*

12 NEW STATIONS FOR OLD

Above: While BR has been noted for vast numbers of station closures during the 1950s and 60s a few new stations have been built as for example Bristol Parkway, an out of town location conveniently placed on the Bristol and South Wales to London and North of England rail routes and strategically near the interchange between the M4 and M5 motorways. It was designed with a large amount of car-parking space to attract car users from Bristol and district to use the train for the major part of their journey. Since this picture was taken an extended canopy has been provided to give wet weather coverage for passengers. *British Railways*

Below: A class 86 electric locomotive is framed in one of the doorways of the entrance to the former booking hall of old Euston, photographed at a time when the original station was still under reconstruction into the modern structure of today which was not completed until 1968 a few years after electrification. *G M Kichenside*

Above: Down the road from Euston, Kings Cross station was given a much less ambitious modernisation by construction of a new concourse along the station frontage including ticket hall, refreshment room, reception area and taxi rank.

G R Mortimer

Below: Rebuilding of many local stations has also been carried out although not all as extensive as at Hatfield where the station has been completely rebuilt on the down side to allow the easing of a curve on the main lines to permit higher speeds. Here Peak class 46 No 182 passes Hatfield with an up express for Kings Cross on 29 July 1972.

Roland Hummerston

13 SIGNALLING FOR SPEED

Above: A feature of BR modernisation has been the wholesale resignalling with colour-light signals, full track circuiting, the automatic track to train warning system at signals and, above all, centralised control of the signalling from new power signalling centres which supervise in some cases as much as 100 miles or more of line from control panels such as this. Merely by pressing a pair of buttons the signalman can set a route for a train 50 miles away and can see its location by a line of red lights on his track diagram together with an indication of its identity by code letters and numbers displayed in the apertures along the track diagram. This particular panel is at Saltley near Birmingham. *British Railways*

Top right: After the commissioning of new signalling special test trains run up and down the lines concerned to ensure that the signals are in fact working correctly to supplement the electrical tests made in the signalbox relay room. This is a train at Harrow & Wealdstone in 1964 testing the new up fast main line signalling controlled by Watford power signalbox instead of the old Harrow No 1 illustrated here. In front of the train is the aws magnet for the next signal ahead. *G M Kichenside*

Bottom right: Typical BR colour-light signals including on the right-hand side a signal with a junction indicator. *D E Canning*

Below: Some of the new signalling also affects motorists at level crossings where automatic half-barriers and traffic signals initiated by the approach of a train have replaced many rural manned level crossings with swing gates. As far as possible on high-speed lines level crossings will be eliminated altogether. *British Railways*

14 AIR-CONDITIONED COMFORT

Above: A feature of a growing number of Inter-City trains from the late 1960s onwards has been the provision of full air-conditioning on ordinary coaches. Until then air-conditioning had been used on the one or two luxury Pullman trains and BR is one of the few railway administrations in the world, particularly in temperate climates, to have such high standards of passenger comfort on ordinary non-supplement services. Some other railways run a few specially selected expresses with such facilities but usually charge extra for travel in them.   *P J Fowler*

Left: The interior of an air-conditioned Mark II second class coach. The latest type of BR coach, the Mark III, is longer at 72ft than earlier BR stock and includes an extra eight seats in second class vehicles.   *G F Heiron*

15 IMPROVING THE TRACK

Above: As part of the programme to raise speed limits where possible British Railways have undertaken civil engineering works in many places on principal main lines to ease curves, as for example here at Relly Mill near Durham on the East Coast main line. The newly sited signal stands in the alignment of the old track which has not yet been removed. Deltic diesel No 9005 heads the 11.00 Kings Cross-Newcastle on 14 September 1969. *I S Carr*

Below: At certain principal running junctions BR has installed high-speed points to allow trains on the diverging route to run almost as fast as those on the major line. One of the places where this was carried out was Weaver Junction where the Liverpool line diverges from the main Euston-Glasgow line; the new turnouts allow trains to and from Liverpool to negotiate the junction at 70mph instead of the 90mph on the main line. There is also a flying junction here carrying the up Liverpool line over the up and down route to Glasgow. An English Electric class 40 approaches with a Glasgow-Euston train and nears the convergence of the up Liverpool line, here on the far side adjacent to the signalbox. *Kenneth Field*

16 TRAINS OF TOMORROW

Above: The next generation of express trains for Inter-City service on BR will be based on the High Speed Train prototype seen here passing the Newton Abbot offices of David & Charles, publisher of this book. The unit was on trial in January 1975 over the steeply-graded South Devon main line between Newton Abbot and Plymouth. It consists of a power car at each end of a rake of Mark III coaches which will form set formation trains. The prototype train entered service between London and Bristol in May 1975 and production batches are expected to enter service in 1976/77.

Below: The other new generation of trains is the highly revolutionary Advanced Passenger Train embodying constructional principles derived from aircraft practice for lightness, new suspension systems and body-tilting to provide added passenger comfort since this type of train is designed to run at much higher speeds than conventional trains on existing track. The prototype is powered by gas-turbines but the first production trains for the 1980s are expected to be electrically powered for the Euston-Glasgow West Coast main line. The prototype train pushed up the British Rail speed record to 151mph between Didcot and Reading in August 1975. *British Railways*

BR DIESEL AND ELECTRIC LOCOMOTIVE CLASSIFICATION AND NUMBERING

Present class	New numbers	Old type No	Original numbers	Builder	Wheel arrangement	Horse power
Diesel						
20	001-228	1	{ 8000-8199 }{ 8300-27 }	EE	Bo-Bo	1000
24	001-150	2	5000-5150	BR	Bo-Bo	{ 1160 { 1250
25	001-327	2	{ 5151-99 }{ 7500-7677 }	BR	Bo-Bo	1250
26	001-46	2	5300-46	Birmingham RCW Co	Bo-Bo	1160
27	001-44 }101-112 }201-12	2	5347-5415	Birmingham RCW Co	Bo-Bo	1250
31	001-19 }101-327 }401-22	2	{ 5500-5699 }{ 5800-62 }	Brush Traction	A1A-A1A	1470
33	001-65 }101-19 }201-12	3	6500-97	Birmingham RCW Co	Bo-Bo	1550
37	001-308	3	{ 6600-08 }{ 6700-6999 }	EE	Co-Co	1750
40	001-199	4	200-399	EE	1Co-Co1	2000
44	001-10	4	1-10	BR	1Co-Co1	2300
45	001-77 }101-150	4	11-137	BR	1Co-Co1	2500
46	001-56	4	138-193	BR	1Co-Co1	2500
47	001-555	4	{ 1100-1111 }{ 1500-1999 }	Brush Traction	Co-Co	2600
50	001-50	4	400-49	EE	Co-Co	2700
52	1000-73	4	1000-73	BR	C-C	2700
53	1200	4	0280	Brush Traction	Co-Co	2880
55	001-22	5	9000-21	EE	Co-Co	3300
Electric						
71	001-14	750V dc	E5001-14	BR	Bo-Bo	2552
73	001-6 }101-42	Electro-diesel	E6001-49	BR	Bo-Bo	1600/600
74	001-10	Electro-diesel	E6101-10	BR	Bo-Bo	2552/650
76	001-57	EM1 1500V dc	E26001-57	BR	Bo-Bo	1868
81	001-22	AL1	{ E3001-23 }{ E3096/7 }	AEI	Bo-Bo	3200
82	001-8	AL2	E3047-54	AEI	Bo-Bo	3300
83	001-15	AL3	{ E3024-35 }{ E3098-3100 }	EE	Bo-Bo	2950
84	001-10	AL4	E3036-45	GEC	Bo-Bo	3100
85	001-40	AL5	E3056-95	BR	Bo-Bo	3200
86	001-48 }201-52	AL6	E3101-3200	BR	Bo-Bo	{ 3600 { 4000
87	001-34	—	—	BR	Bo-Bo	5000

This list shows the overall blocks of numbers originally allocated to each class and does not necessarily include individual locomotives withdrawn before new blocks of numbers were allocated later. Locomotives were not necessarily renumbered in order into the new series.

Builders: EE—English Electric Co; AEI—Associated Electrical Industries; GEC—General Electric Co; BR—British Railways Workshops.

Until the end of steam traction in 1968 diesel locomotives carried a prefix letter D in front of the locomotive number.